Ice Cream
The Cold Creamy Treat

Elaine Landau

THE ROURKE PRESS, INC.

VERO BEACH, FLORIDA 32964

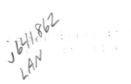

PHOTO CREDITS
Ben Klaffke

EDITORIAL SERVICES
Editorial Directions Inc.

Library of Congress Cataloging-in-Publication Data

Landau, Elaine.
    Ice cream : the cold creamy treat / Elaine Landau.
        p. cm. — (Tasty treats)
    Includes bibliographical references.
    Summary: Provides a brief introduction to ice cream, describing the history of this popular food, different flavors, and
how it can be enjoyed.
    ISBN 1-57103-338-6
    1. Ice cream, ices, etc.—Juvenile literature. [1. Ice cream, ices, etc.] I. Title.

TX795 .L36 2000
641.8'62—dc21

                                                                        00–022396

Printed in the USA

Contents

Ice cream is a cool creamy treat.

Ice Cream

Quick, name a cold creamy dessert. One that tastes good. Did you say ice cream? You are not alone. Millions of people like ice cream.

There are many wonderful ways to eat ice cream.

Ice cream is eaten many different ways. There are ice-cream cones, ice-cream sandwiches, and ice-cream pops. What about ice-cream **sundaes** or ice-cream sodas. Some people like ice cream on top of a piece of warm pie. Others prefer ice-cream cake.

More ice cream is eaten in the United States than anywhere else in the world. One third of all American families eat a gallon of ice cream every two weeks!

You don't have to be a kid to love ice cream.

Early Ice Cream History

Some historians say ice cream dates back to **ancient** Rome. The Emperor Nero supposedly sent workers into the mountains to collect snow. Nero flavored the snow with fruit juice and honey.

Another ice-cream story involves the **explorer** Marco Polo. Marco Polo traveled to China. There he discovered many wonderful things. Ice cream was said to be among them.

King Charles I of England reportedly loved ice cream. He served it at special royal dinners. The king paid a cook a large sum of money to keep the recipe secret.

Some royals used the snow outside their castles to make ice cream.

Ice Cream in America

Ice cream was a hit in the American colonies. It was a favorite of George Washington. Thomas Jefferson liked it, too.

Dolley Madison was the wife of President James Madison. In the early 1800s, she served ice cream at White House balls.

The earliest ice cream was made of fruit flavored snow – much like today's snow cones.

Here an old fashioned ice cream maker is placed next to a modern one.

The first hand-cranked ice-cream churner was made in 1846. It was designed by a New England housewife named Nancy Johnson. She sold her invention for just $200. That was the start of it all. Today, a large ice-cream industry exists.

A family makes ice cream the old fashioned way

Fabulous Flavors

Many different kinds of ice cream are made. Ice cream lovers may choose from flavors such as double dutch chocolate, bubble gum, mint chocolate chip, banana ripple, and cookie dough.

Its green color makes this mint chocolate chip ice cream a good St. Patrick's Day choice.

These are some of the most popular ice cream flavors.

There are also hundreds of other flavors. Some of these are special holiday flavors. Pumpkin ice cream is popular at Thanksgiving and Halloween. Eggnog ice cream is a Christmas treat.

More familiar ice-cream flavors are popular, too. The top ten flavors are:

Vanilla
Chocolate
Butter pecan
Strawberry
Neopolitan
Chocolate chip
French vanilla
Cookies and cream
Vanilla fudge ripple
Praline pecan

Vanilla ice cream has long been the best-seller. Many people like its taste. Vanilla is also often used in sundaes and sodas.

This girl enjoys some vanilla ice cream – the best selling flavor in America

Ice Cream, Ice Cream, Ice Cream!

Ice cream is everywhere. You can buy it in supermarkets. Or find it in ice-cream parlors. Ice cream trucks bring it to neighborhood streets.

These girls enjoy ice cream on a warm summer day.

Supermarkets sell many different kinds of ice cream.

People also make ice cream at home. Ice cream is eaten year-round. More of it is eaten in the summer, however. July is National Ice Cream Month. So do people in warmer parts of the country eat more ice cream? The answer is no.

New Englanders are the biggest ice-cream eaters. They eat about fourteen more pints of ice cream each year than the average American.

Ice cream has long been a popular treat. As the old saying goes:

I scream,
You scream,
We all scream for ice cream!

Just about everybody likes ice cream.

Glossary

ancient (AYN shunt) – existing long ago

explorer (ek SPLOR er) – someone who travels to little-known areas

praline pecan (PRA len pi KAN) – a sugary, pecan ice-cream flavor

sundae (SUN de) – ice cream topped with whipped cream, syrup, nuts, and other things

For Further Reading

Kalbacken, Joan. *The Food Pyramid*. Danbury, Connecticut: Children's Press, 1998.

Knight, Bertram. *From Cow to Ice Cream*. Danbury, Connecticut: Children's Press, 1997.

Patten, Barbara. *Digestion: Food at Work*. Vero Beach, Florida: Rourke, 1996.

Powell, Jillian. *Food and Your Health*. Austin, Texas: Raintree Steck-Vaughn, 1998.

Index